P9-ARQ-276

DISCARD

SOME MAJOR EVENTS IN WORLD WAR II

THE EUROPEAN THEATER

1939 SEPTEMBER—Germany invades Poland; Great Britain, France, Australia, & New Zealand declare war on Germany; Battle of the Atlantic begins. NOVEMBER—Russia invades Finland.

1940 APRIL—Germany invades Denmark & Norway. MAY—Germany invades Belgium, Luxembourg, & The Netherlands; British forces retreat to Dunkirk and escape to England. JUNE—Italy declares war on Britain & France; France surrenders to Germany. JULY—Battle of Britain begins. SEPTEMBER—Italy invades Egypt; Germany, Italy, & Japan form the Axis countries. OCTOBER—Italy invades Greece. NOVEMBER—Battle of Britain over. DECEMBER—Britain attacks Italy in North Africa.

1941 JANUARY—Allies take Tobruk. FEBRUARY—Rommel arrives at Tripoli. APRIL—Germany invades Greece & Yugoslavia. JUNE—Allies are in Syria; Germany invades Russia. JULY—Russia joins Allies. AUGUST—Germans capture Kiev. OCTOBER—Germany reaches Moscow. DECEMBER—Germans retreat from Moscow; Japan attacks Pearl Harbor; United States enters war against Axis nations.

1942 MAY—first British bomber attack on Cologne. JUNE—Germans take Tobruk. SEPTEMBER—Battle of Stalingrad begins. OCTOBER—Battle of El Alamein begins. NOVEMBER—Allies recapture Tobruk; Russians counterattack at Stalingrad.

1943 JANUARY—Allies take Tripoli. FEBRUARY—German troops at Stalingrad surrender. APRIL—revolt of Warsaw Ghetto Jews begins. MAY—German and Italian resistance in North Africa is over; their troops surrender in Tunisia; Warsaw Ghetto revolt is put down by Germany. JULY—allies invade Sicily; Mussolini put in prison. SEPTEMBER—Allies land in Italy; Italians surrender; Germans occupy Rome; Mussolini rescued by Germany. OCTOBER—Allies capture Naples; Italy declares war on Germany. NOVEMBER—Russians recapture Kiev.

1944 JANUARY—Allies land at Anzio. JUNE—Rome falls to Allies; Allies land in Normandy (D-Day). JULY—assassination attempt on Hitler fails. AUGUST—Allies land in southern France. SEPTEMBER—Brussels freed. OCTOBER—Athens liberated. DECEMBER—Battle of the Bulge.

1945 JANUARY—Russians free Warsaw. FEBRUARY—Dresden bombed. APRIL—Americans take Belsen and Buchenwald concentration camps; Russians free Vienna; Russians take over Berlin; Mussolini killed; Hitler commits suicide. MAY—Germany surrenders; Goering captured.

THE PACIFIC THEATER

1940 SEPTEMBER—Japan joins Axis nations Germany & Italy.

1941 APRIL—Russia & Japan sign neutrality pact. DECEMBER—Japanese launch attacks against Pearl Harbor, Hong Kong, the Philippines, & Malaya; United States and Allied nations declare war on Japan; China declares war on Japan, Germany, & Italy; Japan takes over Guam, Wake Island, & Hong Kong; Japan attacks Burma.

1942 JANUARY—Japan takes over Manila; Japan invades Dutch East Indies. FEBRUARY—Japan takes over Singapore; Battle of the Java Sea. APRIL—Japanese overrun Bataan. MAY—Japan takes Mandalay; Allied forces in Philippines surrender to Japan; Japan takes Corregidor; Battle of the Coral Sea. JUNE—Battle of Midway; Japan occupies Aleutian Islands. AUGUST—United States invades Guadalcanal in the Solomon Islands.

1943 FEBRUARY—Guadalcanal taken by U.S. Marines. MARCH—Japanese begin to retreat in China. APRIL—Yamamoto shot down by U.S. Air Force. MAY—U.S. troops take Aleutian Islands back from Japan. JUNE—Allied troops land in New Guinea. NOVEMBER—U.S. Marines invade Bougainville & Tarawa.

1944 FEBRUARY—Truk liberated. JUNE—Saipan attacked by United States. JULY—battle for Guam begins. OCTOBER—U.S. troops invade Philippines; Battle of Leyte Gulf won by Allies.

1945 JANUARY—Luzon taken; Burma Road won back. MARCH—Iwo Jima freed. APRIL—Okinawa attacked by U.S. troops; President Franklin Roosevelt dies; Harry S. Truman becomes president. JUNE—United States takes Okinawa. AUGUST—atomic bomb dropped on Hiroshima; Russia declares war on Japan; atomic bomb dropped on Nagasaki. SEPTEMBER—Japan surrenders.

DISCARD

WORLD AT WAR

Siege of
Leningrad

DISCARD

WORLD AT WAR

Siege of Leningrad

By R. Conrad Stein

Consultant:
Professor Robert L. Messer, Ph.D.
Department of History
University of Illinois at Chicago

 CHILDRENS PRESS, CHICAGO

45530

Adolf Hitler (second from right) and Benito Mussolini
(fourth from left) take a tour of inspection of the Eastern Front
in September, 1941, not long after Germany invaded Russia.

FRONTISPIECE: A German rider
gallops through a burning Russian town
during the early weeks of the German
invasion of Russia.

Library of Congress Cataloging in Publication Data

Stein, R. Conrad.
  The siege of Leningrad

  (World at war)
  Includes index.
  Summary: Describes the nearly 900-day siege of the
Baltic port city of Leningrad, during which more than
one million Russian civilians died from starvation,
cold, and German shells.
    1. Leningrad (R.S.F.S.R.)—Siege, 1941–1944—
Juvenile literature. 2. World War, 1939–1945—
Campaigns—Soviet Union—Juvenile literature.
[1. Leningrad (R.S.F.S.R.)—Siege, 1941–1944.
2. World War, 1939–1945—Campaigns—Soviet
Union]
  I. Title. II. Series.
D764.3.L4S83 1983   947'.453   82-17841
ISBN 0-516-04773-6

Copyright © 1983 by Regensteiner Publishing
Enterprises, Inc. All rights reserved. Published
simultaneously in Canada. Printed in the United
States of America.
  2 3 4 5 6 7 8 9 10 R 92 91 90 89 88 87 86 85 84 83

PICTURE CREDITS:
WIDE WORLD PHOTOS: Pages, 6, 8, 9,
16, 21, 22, 25, 26, 28, 30, 33, 34, 35, 36,
39, 40, 43, 46
UPI: Cover, pages 4, 11, 12, 13, 14, 15,
17, 18, 38, 41, 42, 44
Len Meents (Map): Page 10

COVER PHOTO: Women members of
Leningrad's fire-fighting service keep
watch over the city.

PROJECT EDITOR:
Joan Downing

CREATIVE DIRECTOR:
Margrit Fiddle

On June 22, 1941, all of Europe seemed to hold its breath. The mighty German army was crossing yet another border. The Germans had already conquered Poland, France, Denmark, Norway, Yugoslavia, Greece, and much of northern Africa. Now they were invading their immense neighbor to the east—Russia.

Both Russia and Germany were led by ruthless dictators. In Russia, Joseph Stalin was the Supreme Soviet Commander. For years, Stalin and Adolf Hitler had played a confusing friend-enemy game. In 1939, they signed a non-aggression pact and divided Poland between them. They mistrusted each other, however, and knew their armed truce was only temporary. Now Hitler believed that if he were able to defeat Stalin, his remaining enemies would fall quickly. Hitler would then become the master of Europe.

This column of German tanks continued their swift
advance across Russia after leaving a village in flames.

In the opening weeks of battle, it appeared
that nothing could stop the Germans. Their
armies streaked across Russia with lightning
speed. Columns of tanks sometimes ten to fifteen
miles long struck deep into Soviet territory. In
just two weeks, almost one million Russian
soldiers had been trapped by giant encircling
movements. After a month of fighting, many
German generals believed the war was as good
as won.

Above: German infantry, supported by motorized units, attacked this Russian village four days after the invasion.
Below: On that same day, June 26, the city of Minsk fell to the Germans.

The German offensive had three targets. Each
lay hundreds of miles inside Russian territory.
To the south, the Germans wanted to occupy
the land area of the Ukraine and the Caucasus
Mountains. In the center of the front, the
German Army drove for the capital city of
Moscow. To the north, the Germans hoped to
conquer another important city—Leningrad.

The city of Leningrad held three million
people. It was a vital port on the Baltic Sea and
the second largest city in Russia. As the German
Army rolled closer during that summer of 1941,

All able-bodied Leningrad citizens helped in the effort to defend
their city. These women spent days digging antitank trenches on the
outskirts of Leningrad. Others built bunkers and set up antitank obstacles.

the people of Leningrad dug tank traps and
strung barbed wire. But while they worked,
Leningraders felt bitter. For years they had been
told that their Red Army was invincible. Now
their army was crumbling before the onrushing
Germans. Leningrad's commander, General Ivan
Fedyuninsky, approached one elderly woman
who was helping to dig a trench on the outskirts
of Leningrad. "You are digging well," the
general said. The woman stopped her digging for
a moment. "Yes," she said. "We are digging
well, but you fellows are fighting badly."

Much of the blame for the Red Army's failure to stop the onrushing Germans could be laid to Joseph Stalin. The Soviet leader was a lonely man who was insanely protective of his power. In the years before World War II, Stalin had ordered people shot—first by the hundreds, then by the thousands. Those executed were Russians whom Stalin believed were his enemies. Many of Stalin's real or imagined enemies were army officers. From lieutenants to generals, Red Army officers were lined up against walls and shot by firing squads. The mass executions demoralized the army and left the soldiers without leadership.

Soviet soldiers, fighting against the odds, charge up a
grass-covered slope to storm nearby German positions.

But though the Red Army's officer corps was
disorganized, the Germans were surprised to
discover that the Russian soldier was a tough
fighting man. "The conduct of Russian troops,"
wrote German General Guenther Blumentritt,
"was in striking contrast to the Poles and the
Western Allies in defeat. Even when encircled
the Russians stood their ground and fought."
When attacking, the Russian foot soldier
shrieked a fierce battle cry: *"Uurah! Uurah!
Uurah!"*

Georgi K. Zhukov (right) was appointed military commander for the northern front in September, 1941.

Still the German juggernaut advanced. In just two months, German armored units in the north ripped through five hundred miles of Russian territory. By September of 1941, the Germans were assailing the outskirts of Leningrad. Then, when the collapse of the city seemed certain, Stalin appointed a new military commander for the northern front. His name was Georgi K. Zhukov.

By September, the Germans had reached the suburbs of Leningrad (above). Antiaircraft gunners in camouflage capes (below) were stationed on the outskirts of Leningrad to keep watch for German planes.

A Red Army officer reviews a unit of the Leningrad People's Volunteer Force.

Marshal Zhukov was a hard-driving general who had escaped the Stalin-ordered executions of the late 1930s. He was in charge of the northern front for only four weeks. But his leadership in that short time shocked the men into action. Zhukov's military philosophy was simple. He insisted that his troops attack, attack, and attack again. When he took over, the Russian divisions were low on food. Many of his troops had rifles, but there were few bullets. Some of his men did not even have rifles. All this made little difference to Zhukov. He ordered an immediate attack on all fronts. Thousands of Russians charged the Germans and were gunned down by machine guns and artillery. Zhukov simply ordered his men to regroup and attack again. *"Uurah! Uurah!"*

At the suburbs of Leningrad, the mighty German army was finally stopped.

Finnish bicycle troops enter a captured Russian village.

There were several reasons why the German army did not take Leningrad in 1941. Certainly the fierce Russian resistance was a major reason. But also Hitler believed that a city surrounded was better than a city captured. To the north of Leningrad, the Finnish army was firmly entrenched. Finland had been fighting the Russians since 1939. The Germans held all other roads, rail lines, and bridges that led into the city. They also held the important ports on the

Baltic. So supplying Leningrad by sea from the west would be impossible. In a speech on November 8, 1941, Adolf Hitler said, "Leningrad's hands are in the air. It falls sooner or later. No one can free it. No one can break the ring. Leningrad is doomed to die of famine."

In late 1941, the first military battles for Leningrad wound down. But the siege of Leningrad was just beginning.

A siege is the act of surrounding an enemy strongpoint in hopes of starving it into submission. Besieging a city is an ancient tactic in warfare. Thousands of years ago, the Greeks surrounded Troy and besieged that city for ten years. For civilians, a city besieged is the cruelest form of warfare. What little food exists in a blockaded city usually goes to the soldiers. The rest of the people starve.

Leningrad was a city rich in both beauty and history. It had been founded in 1703 by the Russian emperor Peter the Great. He called the city St. Petersburg. Peter built his new city with broad boulevards, parks, fountains, and statues. The city was renamed Leningrad when the communist hero V. I. Lenin died in 1924. By then Leningrad had become an important cultural center. There were many universities and the city boasted the highest student population in Russia. Writers, artists, musicians, and actors also congregated there. Many Leningraders were freethinkers, just the kind of people Joseph Stalin hated and feared. Hundreds of Leningrad citizens were gunned down during Stalin's mass executions.

In 1941 the first snows fell on Leningrad in October.

Leningrad is as far north as Anchorage, Alaska. The people had long been accustomed to brutal winters. But the winter of 1941-42 was one of the most bitter on record. The temperatures averaged nine degrees above zero in December, and four degrees below zero in

The beautiful city of Leningrad, as it looked before the siege

January. Every day, icy winds howled out of the north and swept the city. First the people burned up all their kerosene. Next the coal ran out. Then they burned furniture, park benches, porch steps, anything they could find. Finally there was nothing left to burn.

Leningraders started dying in November. Families used children's sleds to drag the frozen corpses of their relatives to mass graves. At first, Leningraders were shocked to see someone dragging a sled bearing a frozen body through their streets. Later, that gruesome sight became common in their city.

The winter of 1941–42 was the coldest in half a century. Many of these workers, weakened by hunger and cold, could hardly lift the shovels they were using to clear the snow that blocked Leningrad's main street.

Starvation is a slow, creeping death. A rumbling stomach is just the first sign. After several days without food, a starving person feels a sense of gloom so dark it cannot be described. Next the weakness sets in. The staircase he used to climb easily suddenly becomes too steep to climb at all. Soon distressing bodily changes become noticeable. Arms and legs shrivel up and begin to look like sticks. There is a constant feeling of tiredness. "Today it is simple to die," wrote a Leningrad woman named Elena Skrjabina. "You just begin to lose interest, then you lie on the bed and you never get up."

Another woman visited a Leningrad apartment during the first awful winter of the siege and found this: "Frost on the walls. On a chair the corpse of a fourteen-year-old boy. In a cradle the corpse of a tiny child. On the bed the dead mistress of the flat. At the doorway a neighbor looking without comprehension upon the scene. The next day she died, too."

The Russians launched attacks to try to break the blockade. All the attacks were beaten back. Some Russian units suffered 100 percent casualties. The Germans were firmly dug in. Many of their positions were on the opposite side of the Neva River, which snakes through the suburbs of Leningrad. A river is a formidable barrier for attacking troops. The German ring around Leningrad was like iron.

Every day shells from huge German guns pounded the city. Sometimes the shellfire was concentrated on one particular neighborhood. At other times the shells fell at random. In addition to artillery, the German air force rained bombs on the suffering city.

The German high command hoped their allies would destroy Leningrad without the need for an attack. The German's allies were cold, hunger, and terror.

The Soviet generals decided to try to supply Leningrad through one fragile lifeline. To the east of Leningrad spreads the huge Lake Ladoga. The Germans occupied the southern tip of that lake and the Finns the northern. The east and west banks were still in Soviet hands.

In the winter the lake froze solid. Trucks could run over the ice and bring food, fuel, and ammunition to the city. Soviet leaders insisted that most of the food go to the soldiers and workers. The leaders wanted Leningrad's factories to keep operating despite the siege.

A column of trucks crosses the dangerous ice road over Lake Ladoga to bring food to the besieged people of Leningrad.

Communist Party Secretary Andrei Zhdanov was in charge of Leningrad. Zhdanov had the awesome responsibility of parceling out the few tons of food that arrived each day over Lake Ladoga to three million nearly starving people. Zhdanov organized a rationing system. But each week the rations had to be reduced. On November 13, new rations were announced.

Workers were to receive 300 grams of bread a day. That was about half a loaf. Non-workers were allowed 150 grams—about six slices. There were no dairy products, no sugar, no meat. By November 20, the meager rations had to be reduced once more. Non-workers ended up with about three slices of bread a day.

Men and women would do anything for food. Cats and dogs disappeared from the streets. They were killed and eaten. Pigeons and sparrows also disappeared. Even the rats fled the city because they could find no food. People boiled down leather suitcases and shoes to make soup. Some tried to eat bark they stripped off pine trees in the parks. Others tore wallpaper off the walls to eat the glue, which they believed was made from potato flour. Still others ate plaster just to fill their stomachs. Before the war, Leningrad women had enjoyed dressing up for Saturday night dates. During the siege, they ate their lipsticks.

Leningrad children, heavily clothed against the freezing temperatures, sit out an air raid at a shelter in a city park.

Leningraders had once taken pride in their high degree of culture. Theirs was a city of poets and artists. People were interested in the gentle pursuits, and there was little crime in the streets. But the gripping cold, constant hunger, and terror caused by shells and bombs changed all that. Vicious gangs roamed the streets. Many gang members were soldiers who had deserted the front lines. The gangs broke into bread shops to steal food. They murdered people in their apartments and stole anything they could drag out.

A new type of crime quickly spread in the besieged city. In order to receive a daily bread ration, each Leningrader had to have a ration card. New ration cards were issued on the first of each month. Gang members and pickpockets stole the precious cards. A thriving black market began in counterfeit ration cards. One woman, who worked in a shop that printed the cards, was found to have one hundred ration cards in her purse. She was shot by a firing squad.

But while some turned to crime, hundreds of other Leningraders behaved in a remarkably civilized manner. A Communist Party official named Pavlov told this story: "The driver of a truck was delivering loaves of bread to a bakery when a shell hit the front of the truck and killed the driver.... The loaves of bread were scattered over the pavement. Conditions were favorable for looting. Yet the people who gathered round the wrecked vehicle raised the alarm and guarded the bread till the arrival of another truck. All these people were hungry, and the temptation to grab a fresh loaf of bread was well-nigh irresistible. And yet not a single loaf was stolen."

City officials even managed to keep the schools open during the blockade. A schoolgirl named Luba Tereshchenkova told how difficult it was to do classroom work during the first winter of the blockade: "It was agony to stand up and go to the blackboard.... At the blackboard it was so cold and dark, and your hand, imprisoned in its heavy glove, went all numb and rigid and refused to obey. The chalk kept falling out of your hand, and the lines were all crooked...."

These children, lucky enough to be evacuated from Leningrad during the siege, learned to help a collective farmer in a field in the Kirov region.

Throughout the winter of 1941-42, Leningrad depended on the trucks carrying supplies over frozen Lake Ladoga. On their return trips, the trucks carried non-working civilians out of the city so there would be fewer mouths to feed. The weaker people were evacuated first. They had to sit for up to ten hours on the freezing back of a truck. Many people froze to death while riding on trucks that were meant to rescue them.

Although the trucks flowed in endless columns back and forth across the lake, they still could not bring in enough food to feed the people. On January 5, 1942, Party Secretary Andrei Zhdanov wrote: "The road brings to Leningrad not more than one-third the freight needed for survival even on the scantiest level of existence. The people are suffering unbelievable hardships."

The death count from hunger, cold, and bombardment increased as the siege continued.

Eleven thousand people died in November. Five times that many died in December. By January, at least four thousand Leningraders a day were dying. The sub-zero weather turned the ground to an iron hardness. It became impossible to bury the dead fast enough. The bodies lay in nightmarish piles near the cemeteries.

In late January, one reporter wrote of Leningrad: "The city is dead. There is no electricity. No trams [streetcars]. No water. Almost the only kind of transport is sleds, carrying corpses. The city is dying as it has lived for the last half year—clenching its teeth."

But somehow the city survived the winter. And spring finally came.

In Leningrad's many parks, spring buds began appearing on the tree branches. But for many Leningraders, the streetcars were the most welcome sight. To save fuel, the streetcar lines had been shut down since fall. Now the city leaders had ordered the noisy metal monsters to run once more. From all over the city came the cry, "The trams are running! The trams are

During that first wretched winter, in a city with no fuel, almost no
food, and frozen water mains, everyone "made do." These Leningraders,
taking advantage of a broken main in a city street, used any
kind of container that was handy to dip up some of the precious water.

Party Secretary Andrei Zhdanov (right) stayed in the city and worked for the people of Leningrad.

running!" One German prisoner of war told his Russian guards that he lost faith in Hitler the moment he saw streetcars rumbling over the streets of Leningrad.

There were other spring miracles. Museums opened. A few movie houses unlocked their doors. The symphony orchestra gave a concert. People on the streets actually smiled again.

Leningraders also hailed a new hero. Many high Communist officials had bribed truck drivers to carry them out of the city during the winter. But Party Secretary Zhdanov stayed and worked for the people and suffered with them. Soon posters with Zhdanov's picture were seen

pasted on buildings. Practically nowhere in
Leningrad could one find a picture of Joseph
Stalin. Leningraders knew he was no friend of
their city.

Zhdanov ordered a spring cleaning for the
entire city. Leningraders were eager to pitch in.
But their efforts were quickly frustrated by
German artillery. During the winter, the
Germans had moved enormous railway guns to
the perimeter surrounding the city. Some of
those guns could hurl a one-thousand-pound
shell a distance of twenty miles. While the
coming of spring brought sunlight to Leningrad,
it also brought increased shelling.

Above: Effects of German shellfire on a Leningrad tram
Below: The imposing Peterhof Palace, as it looked before
being devasted by German shells and bombs.

In the summer of 1942, the Germans renewed their offense on the Russian front. This time they concentrated their efforts in the south, where German tanks were driving toward Stalingrad, a city on the Volga River. In the north, the Germans were content to tighten their iron grip around Leningrad. Day after day, shells from their big guns ripped into the city. The summer vanished into fall while battles raged and big guns thundered.

Soon Leningrad entered its second winter of siege.

The winter of 1942-43 was another bitter one for the people of the surrounded city. But they had more food and fuel than they had had the previous winter. When Lake Ladoga froze over in November, Russian engineers accomplished an amazing feat. They laid a railroad track over the thick ice. Supplies were brought to the city on freight cars. During the summer, supplies had been hauled to Leningrad on barges.

Women in Leningrad worked at many jobs during the siege. These two firefighters served at an observation post overlooking the city.

In January of 1943, the Red Army launched a massive winter offensive in the north. A huge force struck the rear of the ring that encircled Leningrad. The Russian army had grown powerful and confident after almost two years of war. The Soviet attack was backed by some 4,500 heavy guns. Also blasting German positions were the frightening Russian multibarreled rocket launchers called Katyushas. The Germans called them "Stalin's pipe organs." A unit of Katyushas could send hundreds of rockets whooshing into the air in the

The massive Red Army winter offensive of 1943 was backed by heavy guns, rocket launchers, and tanks. The Russian soldiers shown above, stationed at the Leningrad front, are armed with long antitank rifles. The infantrymen shown below, mounted on tanks, await the order to advance.

This is the battlefield on the banks of the Neva River where Russian troops broke the German siege ring at Leningrad on January 18, 1943.

span of one minute. Behind the artillery and the rockets came the tough Russian T-34 tanks and wave after wave of Russian foot soldiers. They waded into German positions shouting their chilling battle cry, *"Uurah! Uurah!"*

On January 18, 1943, a Russian tank-infantry column pierced the German ring and joined forces with the Leningrad defenders. A land corridor to Leningrad finally was opened on the 506th day of the blockade. But it was only a corridor, and a narrow one at that. Few supplies

could go through the corridor because it was
constantly bombarded by German artillery. At
other points, the German ring around the city
was as firm as ever. So the German blockade,
though leaking, continued its grip on Leningrad.

The major battle in Russia that winter was
fought far to the south. At Stalingrad on the
Volga, the Germans suffered a defeat from which
they never recovered. After Stalingrad, the
German armies in most of Russia began a long,
painful retreat.

Leningrad children, wounded in the German shelling and bombing, were cared for in the Leningrad Children's Hospital.

But in the north, German artillery shells continued to tear into Leningrad. It seemed as if the Germans wanted to make Leningrad pay for their defeats elsewhere in Russia. July and August of 1943 brought the city the worst shelling of the war. Whole neighborhoods were destroyed. Thousands of lives were lost. Signs appeared on the sides of the downtown buildings:

CITIZENS—IN CASE OF SHELLING,

THIS SIDE OF THE STREET

IS THE MOST DANGEROUS

These Red Army reserves marched through Leningrad in January of 1944 to take part in the battles that finally liberated the city from the German siege.

Somehow the courageous people of Leningrad endured the shelling, just as they had endured the freezing cold and the starvation rations.

In the middle of January 1944, the Red Army launched another massive winter offensive. A Russian cannon barrage roared with so much power that the very ground under Leningrad trembled. Fire-tailed Katyusha rockets whooshed out of thousands of rocket tubes. Monster tanks followed by infantry rolled into German lines. *"Uurah! Uurah! Uurah!"*

This is one of the huge siege guns used by the Germans to shell Leningrad.

By January 27, a rocket salute over Leningrad proclaimed the city to be free once more. After almost nine hundred days, the siege of Leningrad had ended.

People who have lived through a war know that war is both a tragic waste and a form of madness. But the siege of Leningrad exceeded all limits of tragedy and madness. In two and a half years, more than a million people died there. It is nearly impossible to imagine death in such numbers. Never before had a large city endured such suffering and death.

After the war, Zhdanov announced a plan to restore Leningrad to the marvelous city of broad boulevards and green parks that it once had been. But Stalin was jealous of Zhdanov's popularity and growing power. Zhdanov died under mysterious circumstances in 1948. Shortly after his death, many of Zhdanov's friends and associates disappeared. Leningrad became the last of the war-torn Russian cities to be rebuilt. Stalin knew he had enemies there. He hoped the world would forget the struggle of the surrounded city and the men and women who had become heroes during the ordeal.

But history would always remember the courage of three million people. On a stone at the Piskarevsky Cemetery in Leningrad, there is etched a poem dedicated to the memory of the people who died during the siege. The last line of the poem reads:

Let no one forget, let nothing be forgotten.

Index

Page numbers in boldface type indicate illustrations.

About the Author

Mr. Stein was born and grew up in Chicago. At eighteen he enlisted in the Marine Corps where he served three years. He was a sergeant at discharge. He later received a B.A. in history from the University of Illinois and an M.F.A. from the University of Guanajuato in Mexico.

Although he served in the Marines, Mr. Stein believes that wars are a dreadful waste of human life. He agrees with a statement once uttered by Benjamin Franklin: "There never was a good war or a bad peace." But wars are all too much a part of human history. Mr. Stein hopes that some day there will be no more wars to write about.